W9-BHS-713

DUE DATE

TRACKING
THE
FACTS

How to Develop Research Skills

by Claire McInerney
illustrations by Harry Pulver

Lerner Publications Company ▪ Minneapolis

*My grateful thanks to my faithful
research assistant Catherine Fleischman.*

Library of Congress Cataloging-in-Publication Data

McInerney, Claire Fleischman.
Tracking the facts: how to develop research skills / by
Claire McInerney; illustrations by Harry Pulver.
p.   cm. − (Study skills)
Includes bibliographical references.
Summary: Discusses how to develop research skills, including how
to use the public library, how to interview people, how to do
computer searches, and how to organize, outline, and write up one's
research results.
ISBN 0-8225-2426-0 (lib. bdg.)
1. Report writing−Juvenile literature. 2. Study, Method of−
Juvenile literature. [1. Report writing. 2. Research. 3. Study,
Method of.] I. Pulver, Harry, ill. II. Title. III. Series: Study
skills (Minneapolis, Minn.)
LB1047.3.M37   1990

808′.02−dc20   90-5454
                                                                                CIP
                                                                                 AC

Manufactured in the United States of America

1 2 3 4 5 6 7 8 9 10 99 98 97 96 95 94 93 92 91 90

Contents

Introduction **5**

1 Getting Started **9**
    Finding a Topic
    Narrowing the Topic

2 Scoping out Your Research Topic **19**
    Indexes
    Interviewing
    Research Plan

3 Using Information Gold Mines **35**
    Primary and Secondary Sources
    Computerized Searching

4 Getting Ready to Write **45**
    Creating an Outline
    Taking Notes
    Bibliography/Mediagraphy

5 Putting It All Together **57**

Research Timeline **61**

Bibliography **63**

Index **64**

Introduction

Research. It's like going on a treasure hunt, doing detective work, or solving a puzzle. Research is finding out about something really important, even when the subject is unfamiliar at first. You may start learning about something new by asking your family and friends, but eventually, if you are serious about tracking down information, you must become a **researcher**!

Yes, a researcher can be an everyday person, and you can be a researcher if you know the right skills. The difference between just finding an answer to a question and doing research is that research helps you learn a lot about one single subject. Through careful study and hard work, *you* can become an expert about one area of knowledge.

Sometimes kids know more than adults about certain things: stamp collecting, taking care of cats, or writing a computer program, for example. Spending time with stamps, cats, and computers is one way to get to know them well, but genuine experts also study the history of their chosen subject, investigate other people's ideas about it, and read about it.

Using Research to Start a Team

This book is mainly about information **research projects** for school. It will help you determine your research topic and show you how to uncover the best information to research a subject. It will also give you ideas about how to organize and write your research report.

In junior high or high school, research projects are often assigned in English, history, biology, or other classes. You may be wondering how a research project differs from other kinds of projects, such as a science fair demonstration. An information research project is different from a science project, because information research requires a lot of reading, writing, and asking questions. Science research usually requires experiments as well.

Not all research projects are for school, though. Here's an example of a real research project. Cindy wanted to start a girls' basketball team. She had seen basketball on TV, and her brothers played on a high school team, but her middle school had no after-school basketball team.

Cindy thought for a long time about starting a basketball team before she came up with a plan. Cindy began her basketball research by talking to her brothers and their coach. She wrote down all the things they said were necessary for a successful team. She knew that Bob Brown, a friend of her father's, was a retired basketball pro who lived in town. Even though it took a lot of courage, she called Mr. Brown and asked him questions. Next, Cindy went to the school library and made a list of magazines that had articles about basketball. She went to the public library

and found a sports encyclopedia, which listed the offic
rules of the game and the exact measurements of tl
court. She also checked out some sports magazines and
read stories about women's basketball teams.

Now Cindy had enough information to get down to business. The next day at school, she obtained permission from the principal to put a small survey in the school newspaper asking girls and their parents if they would be interested in a Saturday basketball league. Cindy and her friends visited the YMCA, the YWCA, and the local grade school, high school, and community college to see what kind of gym space was available and how much it would cost. They also scoured the town newspaper for ideas about sponsors—local businesses that might help them buy uniforms.

The girls' hard work paid off. The surveys showed that there were enough girls to form six teams. They also found out that they could use the community college gym at no cost on Saturday mornings, and that several parents would volunteer to serve as coaches and referees. The girls' basketball team was on its way. The next research project for Cindy was to find the most awesome basketball shoes.

You Can Do It Too

Cindy had a research problem—how could she organize a girls' basketball team? Through study, interviews, surveys, and personal contacts, she found the answers to all of her technical and special questions. Although research projects are often assigned as schoolwork, research can also help you solve problems and get things done.

Getting Started

Professional writers say that what scares them most about writing is facing a blank piece of paper. Getting started may be the toughest part of a research project for you, too. Does it seem like a big, brain-breaker job? Take it piece by piece—you'll get the job done, and you'll learn that research can be fun.

Bright Ideas through Brainstorming

You can trick yourself into getting started by **brainstorming** some good ideas. Taking your brain by storm means letting yourself think up crazy, wild ideas, as many ideas as you can. You've got to write the ideas down; otherwise they'll disappear. It's more fun to brainstorm in a group, but you can do it by yourself on a sheet of paper.

Here are the rules for brainstorming:
- Speak and write down the very first things that come to mind.
- Don't decide whether ideas are good or bad until later.
- Be as wild as possible—creative ideas can be tamed down, but it is hard to liven up dull ones.

- Be patient with pauses or silences—sometimes the best ideas come right after a pause.
- If you're in a group, don't comment on the ideas until later.
- Feel free to expand on ideas—a good idea doesn't have to be totally new. You can work from ideas already written down to make them more interesting.

Suppose your teacher announces that you will be learning about research methods in school, and you can choose any research topic that you wish. This seems even harder than if your teacher picked the topic for you! It leaves the world of ideas wide open. You start to think about cars, though, since that is your favorite subject. A brainstorming session with two friends might produce this list:

model cars	race cars	cable cars
classic cars	convertibles	car sick
history of cars	car plants or factories	car phones
electric cars	remote-controlled cars	limousines
cattle cars	railroad cars	taxicabs
bumper cars	car wash	Corvettes
foreign cars	junker cars	steering wheels
batmobile	stock car races	customized cars
4-wheelers	police cars	seat belt

The list isn't organized, and the subjects aren't in any order. They're just words that came to mind when you decided to brainstorm on the topic of cars. Any of the topics could turn into an interesting research project. You could find experts, magazine articles, books, or sections of books that talk about each subject.

THE HISTORY OF ALL FOOD

Beware the Monstrous Topic

It is very important to try on your subject for size. It needs to be large enough so that you can find information about it. It also must be small enough so that it does not overwhelm you.

Save yourself from the monster topic by narrowing your topic early. *Don't skip this step in your research project!* If your topic is too big, you'll feel like it is overpowering you. If you pick a small piece of a big subject, though, you'll be pleased and proud when you discover the information easily.

11

Let's look at a monster topic like DINOSAURS. The topic towers like a prehistoric giant over the researcher. Even "dinosaurs of North America" is a huge subject. Whole books have been written about those dinosaurs. Instead, try researching **sauropods**, the the class of dinosaurs that had long necks, long tails, solid bones, and broad feet. What did they eat? How did they live? What did they look like? How did they differ from other dinosaurs? These are all questions you could ask when digging for information.

It is possible to choose a topic that is so narrow that the average student would have a hard time finding enough printed information in a school or small public library to do a research paper. For example, it is interesting that the **segisaurus**, a rabbit-sized dinosaur that lived in Arizona, had solid bones instead of hollow bones like some other dinosaurs. But it might be tough to find enough information about this one dinosaur to make a whole report. It would be fun to investigate tiny dinosaurs, though, and to discover if any animals living today are relatives of the small dinosaurs.

an OK topic	a BETTER topic
Bread Baking through History	The History of the Tortilla
South Africa	A Student's Life in South Africa
Air Pollution	The Effects of Acid Rain on Forests

Chapter 1: Research Skill Activities

Here are four different ways to develop ideas and narrow your research topic. You may want to use all of these suggestions or just one or two.

1. Webbing

Take one of the topics from the car brainstorming list. On a blank piece of paper, quickly write down any ideas related to the topic that come to mind. Don't stop to judge the words you write; just get them on paper. Then connect the words that seem to be related with straight lines. This is your **idea web** from which you can make an outline for your research project.

Here's an example of an idea web for "seat belt":

14

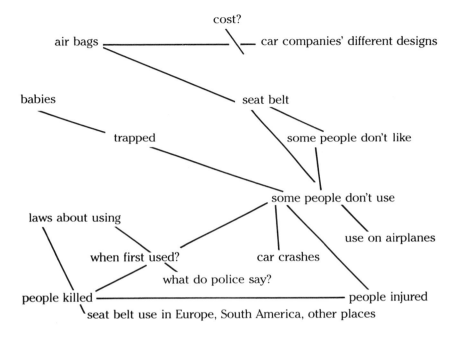

2. Using the encyclopedia

The next step is to track your ideas with expert information. Look in a reference book such as an **encyclopedia** to learn more about your topic. The encyclopedia is a set of 20-30 books that explain something about almost all subjects. If you like dinosaurs and think you might want to write a research report on some aspect of dinosaurs, first read an article about them in the encyclopedia. The encyclopedia can show you how the information about a subject area is organized, as well as how many subtopics there are under one big topic heading.

15

Find the encyclopedia **index** (usually the last volume of the encyclopedia). The index will list the general topic DINOSAURS and give the volumes and page numbers for the information. Think about narrowing your topic to either theropods (two-legged meat eaters) or sauropods (four-legged plant eaters). For a report on seat belts, look in the index under automobile, car, safety, or seat belt.

3. Narrowing the topic

Many students like to learn about different kinds of careers. *Scientist* is too big a topic to cover in one class research report. Consider researching the life and work of a *paleontologist* (a scientist who learns about the past life of our planet by studying fossils). Your research questions might include:

- What does a paleontologist do?
- How does a paleontologist's work differ from an archaeologist's?
- What kind of schooling is needed to study fossils, dinosaurs, and other extinct life forms?
- What is the most fun and what is the hardest part of being a paleontologist?

Think of a career that interests you. Write four questions you could answer in a research report.

4. Mapping or fine-tuning your research questions

After you have made your idea web, have looked up your topic in the encyclopedia, and have narrowed your topic, put the questions that come to mind in an order that makes sense. Writing down your main questions is like drawing a map of your research paper. It shows you what questions need to be researched to give a thorough report. One kind of idea map is an **outline**. An outline lists the major questions with Roman numerals (I, II, III, IV, V, etc.), then uses letters (A, B, C, D, E, etc.) for smaller topics and Arabic numerals (1, 2, 3, 4, 5, etc.) for subtopics (even smaller parts of the larger topic) under the alphabet headings. Here's a sample outline for a research project on seat belts:

SEAT BELTS
I. Introduction
   A. Background—When were seat belts first used?
   B. How do automobile seat belts differ from air bags or airline seat belts?
      1. Research from car companies
      2. Other information
II. How do seat belts save lives?
   A. Car accidents—How do seat belts work in crashes?
   B. What are the facts about seat belt use in car accidents?
      1. Police comments
      2. Facts from other sources
III. What are the laws about seat belt use?
   A. The first seat belt laws—when, where, why?
   B. What similarities are there in laws in the U. S. and Canada?
   C. Do other countries have laws about seat belts?
IV. How will seat belts and other factors contribute to car safety in the future?
   A. Safe traveling for babies and little children
   B. Getting everyone to wear a seat belt
      1. Convincing those who are opposed
      2. Education efforts in schools, TV, radio, and newspapers and magazines

2

Scoping out
Your Research Project

Remember Cindy, who wanted to start a basketball team? She spent time thinking about how to approach the problem. She considered what she needed to read for information, where she had to look for official rules, and whose ideas and opinions she needed. All of Cindy's thinking took place before she did any research about starting a basketball team. Her thinking produced the plan, or **research design**, detailing what action she would take.

Now that *you* have a topic for your research project, it's time to plan your strategy. The research design is a guide to help you decide where to go for the information you need.

Most researchers keep a research log or notebook. Now is a good time for you to start your own research notebook, where you can keep notes about your progress. To decide on a plan of action, ask yourself the following questions. Record your answers in your research notebook.

1. Do I have general knowledge about the subject?

2. What is the general category in which the subject fits?

3. Is this brand-new information or is the subject old enough to be included in books?

4. Would biographies cover this information?

5. Are numbers or facts important to my research?

6. Would someone in my family or neighborhood know something about this subject?

7. Do people strongly disagree about this subject?

8. Do I need to know people's opinions in order to understand this subject?

1. Do I have general knowledge about the subject?

If your answer is YES! move right ahead to the next question. If you have heard of the subject and it sparks some interest, but you know very little about it, start with the encyclopedia in your neighborhood public library or school library/media center. You checked the encyclopedia briefly before to find and narrow your topic. Now you can read about your subject more carefully. Luckily, the subjects are listed in alphabetical order in the encyclopedia, so you can usually dive right into the article you need. Look up your subject in the index too, because there may be a juicy tidbit of information in a place you wouldn't think about at first.

This is a good time to check in with the public librarian and your school library/media person. They will show you where the reference books are located and will help you find other information on your subject. They can also help you use the card catalog or the computer catalog, which tells you where to find all the available books on your topic. You'll save a lot of time and uncover the best material if you ask these information experts for help.

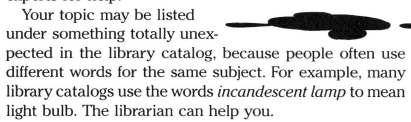

Your topic may be listed under something totally unexpected in the library catalog, because people often use different words for the same subject. For example, many library catalogs use the words *incandescent lamp* to mean light bulb. The librarian can help you.

2. What is the general category in which the subject fits — science? sports? music? government? social problems? medicine? art? food? hobbies? inventions?

Looking up your subject in an encyclopedia is always a good idea, but don't stop there! If you already know about the subject, try finding an article in a special encyclopedia. A big public library will have encyclopedias chock-full of interesting items on a single subject.

Look for the *Encyclopedia of Food* if you want to know about the invention of ice cream. The book *Handtools of Arts and Crafts: The Encyclopedia of the Fine, Decorative and Applied Arts* will tell you all about the tools you need to tie-dye T-shirts. Cindy looked in a sports encyclopedia to find the exact size of a basketball court.

Here's another tip to help you scope out your subject: do some selective browsing. Look up your subject in a library catalog. Write down the **call numbers** (the letters and numbers that appear on the catalog card next to the title and author of a book), which tell you where the books on that subject are located in the library/media center. Find that section and browse. Just as you would browse in the clothing section of a department store to find the right jacket, you can browse for the information that fits your subject.

If the call number has the letter **R** in front of it, the material is probably a reference book. That means the book is housed in the reference section of the library, and you cannot check the book out of the library. If the call number starts with a **J** (juvenile), it might be located in the children's or young people's section of the library. Ask the librarian what the different letters and numbers mean and where the resource material is located.

Useful browsing means that you take the material from the shelf and examine it carefully. If it's a book, look on the back of the title page to see when it was published to find out if the information is current. Look in the index in the back of the book to see if the important subjects in your question outline are covered. Look at the table of contents in the front of the book to see how the book is organized. Read a few paragraphs to see if the writing is clear and easy to understand.

Browsing will help you decide which materials to check out. If the item you found in the catalog is not on the shelf,

ask for help. The librarian may suggest trying to borrow the book from another library. He or she will arrange for an **interlibrary loan**. An interlibrary loan may take a week or two, which is a good reason for starting your project early!

3. Is this brand-new information or is the subject old enough to be included in books?

Here's where your brain goes into action! If the topic is current, that is, in the news recently, written about in news magazines and newspapers, and discussed on TV, there may not be any books written about it yet. A magazine (periodical) index will give you the exact location of the articles you want, right down to the issue of the magazine and the page numbers.

Periodical (magazine) Indexes

The two most common **periodical indexes** used for a school report are *Magazine Index* and *Reader's Guide to Periodical Literature*. Public libraries often have *Magazine Index* on rolls of film called **microfilm**. You can read the film in a special microfilm reader stand. In *Magazine Index* subjects are listed alphabetically, and all the articles on one subject are listed in one place. Of course, you still have to find the article itself and read it or make a photocopy to read later.

Reader's Guide, on the other hand, is published in paperback twice a month. Then, once a year, a large hardcover volume is published with an index of all the articles that appeared in the magazines in one year. When using

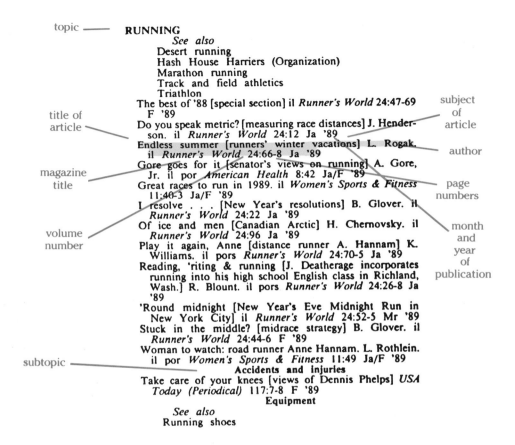

Sample entries from the *Reader's Guide to Periodical Literature*

Reader's Guide, look through the most current paperback issues and then check the less current hardcover books. Your library might not carry all the magazines listed in *Reader's Guide.*

Newspaper Indexes

Most big-city newspapers are indexed, just as magazines are. The *New York Times,* one of the world's most famous newspapers, has its own index, which tells the reader the issue in which an article appeared. Your hometown newspaper may have an index too. Sometimes newspaper indexes are printed in booklet form, but often they are sent to libraries on microfilm or by means of a computer service. You'll probably want to ask the librarian to help you find newspaper articles.

4. Would biographies cover this information?

Subject material may often be found under the names of famous people. A book or film about Abraham Lincoln usually contains information about the United States during the Civil War, for example. In a library, books about peoples' lives are usually shelved together in the **Biography** section. The call number for biographies often starts with a **B**. If the biographies are shelved together, they are filed alphabetically according to the person's last name.

After you read an encyclopedia article about your subject, you may find that there are certain people who are important to your topic. Try to look up information about their lives in biographies or other books for more detailed information. A film or videotape about the life of Martin Luther King, Jr., will give you a good understanding of the civil rights movement in the United States. *The Diary of a Young Girl* by Anne Frank will give you a view of what life was like for a Jewish family in hiding during World War II.

5. Are numbers or facts important to my research?

Sometimes it's important to know the population of a city, the depth of a lake, the climate of a country, or the winner of an Olympic event. If you need a fact for your research report, try the latest issue of an **almanac**. Almanacs are published every year and contain current information about sports, people, government, population, geography, and many other topics. Almanacs are usually located in the reference section of your library.

An almanac is a handy place to find current facts, but there are many other sources of factual information. Informational books, tapes, and films are located in the nonfiction section of the library. Remember that the library catalog lists the call number that will guide you to the material on the shelf. The nonfiction section includes resources about sports, science, history, food, and many other subjects.

6. Would someone in my family or neighborhood know something about this subject?

Asking questions is one of the best ways to gather information. **Interviewing** is the term news reporters use to describe the professional method of asking questions to uncover key facts. It takes skill to be an expert interviewer, but you can become good at it with planning and practice. When you are working on research, tell everyone you meet about your topic. You'll be surprised how often people will say, "You should talk to so-and-so. He knows all about your subject." Write down a list of all your possible sources and find their phone numbers.

7. Do people strongly disagree about this subject?

If your topic is controversial, with strong opinions on both sides of the issue, make sure that you research both sides. Even if you are making a case for or against a course of action (such as capital punishment), you should know the opinions of those who oppose your point of view.

8. Do I need to know people's opinions in order to understand this subject?

If you need information about what people in your school, your community, or your neighborhood think about your topic, you will want to conduct a survey or give out a questionnaire. Cindy used this method when she was trying to prove there was interest in a girls' basketball team and enough players to make it work.

Another method of getting opinions is **polling**—which means you ask a number of different people the same question and write down their answers. You can poll people by calling them on the phone, going door-to-door, or standing in a busy place, such as the school corridor when classes are changing or a shopping mall on a Saturday. Stop people to ask them a series of short questions.

The Big Picture

Now you're ready to write your master plan for research. Here is a simple research plan for a project titled—Running is Excellent Exercise:

Research Plan

Write an outline of questions to answer:

I. What are the advantages and disadvantages of becoming a runner?
   A. Advantages
      1. Exercise
      2. Fresh air
   B. Disadvantages
      1. Injuries
      2. Time commitment
II. What are the health benefits of running?
III. How are the benefits of walking and running different?
IV. What kinds of programs are there for kids who want to become runners?
   A. School
   B. Community
V. What do kids like about running?
   A. Interview results
   B. Survey results

Library work

1. Go to the public library and school media center and talk to the librarian about the topic.

2. Look up running and jogging in an encyclopedia.

3. Look up track, running, walking, and jogging in a sports encyclopedia.

4. Find the subjects jogging or running in the library catalog. After locating the call numbers, browse through the books on the shelves and decide which ones to check out or get through an interlibrary loan.

5. Find a list of magazine articles on walking and jogging

(or running and race walking) in the *Magazine Index* or *Reader's Guide*. Ask the librarian to help you find them.

6. Look in a newspaper index to see if there are any stories about local race-walkers or runners.

Interviews

1. Talk to Mom and Dad to see if they know any experienced runners.

2. Call the high school or junior high track coach to schedule an interview.

3. If possible, call a race-walker or runner to schedule an interview.

4. Visit a local sports store to see if someone will talk about running shoes. The store clerks may also know about local running clubs or groups.

5. Check to see if cassette recorder has batteries that work. Buy two blank cassettes to use when interviewing.

Polling

1. Ask friends what they like about jogging.

2. Stay after school to ask kids on the track team what they like about jogging or running. (Check with the coach first.)

3. Get permission to hand out a survey with questions about walking and jogging.

Take notes at each step.

This is just one example of a research plan that could be used on the subject of running. By mapping out a plan like this one before you begin your information research, you will have a step-by-step guide to accomplishing your tasks. As you check off the items on your plan, you will feel a great sense of getting it together and getting it done. You will learn more about your subject each step of the way.

Chapter 2: Research Skill Activities

1. Buy a pack of 4" x 6" index cards. Now you're ready to make your own "research deck." Write your subject on the first line of one card. Look up your subject in a dictionary. Write the definition on the card.

2. Find the encyclopedias in the library. Find the index to the *Compton's, Colliers,* or *World Book Encyclopedia.* On one of the index cards from your research deck, write the name of the encyclopedia and the volumes and pages that include information about your research topic.

3. Talk to the librarian about your topic. Ask the librarian how you can find your topic in the library catalog.

4. After looking up the subjects in the library catalog, write the call number of each material on another card. Also make note of the name of the item and the author. In case the item isn't on the shelf, you can pull out your research deck and ask the librarian about the item you need. Go to the section that holds the call numbers you wrote down and browse through the books. Find at least two books on your topic that you want to check out of the library.

5. Locate the *Reader's Guide to Periodical Literature.* Is information listed under the subjects *walking* and *running?* Who is the author of an article on walking? What is the title of the article? What magazine published the article? What is the date of the magazine? The page numbers? Does the *Reader's Guide* tell you to see other subjects also? Find the same information (author, article, magazine, issue, page numbers) for a topic you have chosen.

6. After answering the eight questions listed at the beginning of this chapter, complete a research design of your own by writing out the steps you will follow in your project.

7. Keep all your research materials, including your research deck of note cards and the books and magazines that you need, together. It is also a good idea to have a three-ring notebook where you can keep a record of your research progress.

3

Using Information Gold Mines

The Real Thing—Primary Sources

An important part of a thorough research project is to use a **primary source**. A primary source is created when a person witnesses an event at the time it happens and records what he or she observes. Primary sources include diaries, letters, autobiographies, explorers' log books, and ship records. If you wanted to learn when your great-grandparents left Germany to come to the United States or Canada, for example, you might find their names on a ship's log of passengers who sailed from the European seaport of Bremen. Sources such as diaries and letters can be found in historical societies.

If you are doing research on the music group the Rolling Stones, you would be using a primary source if you viewed a film or videotape made at one of the band's concerts. Videotape is becoming an important source of primary material for researchers, since so many current events are recorded and kept on tape.

People as Primary Sources—Interviewing

Assume that there's someone out there whose brain is full of the information you need. Your job is to identify the right source and to track her or him down. An "informant" is an expert on a certain subject who agrees to give an interviewer special information. It may seem very scary to call someone you don't know and ask for an interview. Most people feel flattered that someone has called, though, and nine times out of ten your source will be glad to help out. What have you got to lose? No one will jump out of the phone to zap you! Prepare for your phone call by writing down the information you'll need to set up the interview.

Be honest. Simply say your name, what your project is about, and that you would like to have an interview. Be sure to take notes so you'll know who you'll be talking to, where you'll meet, at what time, and how long you'll have. Ask if you can bring a tape recorder and record your conversation. Once your informant agrees to give you an interview, prepare well.

The Steps Toward a Great Interview

Your first step in interviewing should be to do preliminary library research on your topic, so that you know some basic information about the topic. You want to know enough to ask intelligent questions. Next, prepare a list of questions about your topic. The best interviews are like good conversations, with an easy flow of questions, answers, and ideas. Although you can certainly bring along the list of questions, written neatly in a notebook, it is also

good to have the questions in your mind. Knowing the questions you want to ask ahead of time allows you to relax and to listen carefully to your informant. Being a good listener will automatically trigger other questions that may produce even more interesting answers.

When preparing your questions, think of some that will encourage the informant to talk at length. Stay away from questions that can be answered with one word like "yes" or "no." Here are some examples of good questions:

"Tell me about your life when you lived on the farm."

"What kinds of things did you do for fun when you were a little girl (boy)?"

"How did you learn the skills to become a chef?"

"What are the penalties for using illegal drugs?"

"Please tell me more about that."

"Can you elaborate?"

"What do you mean by the term 'acid rain'?"

"What do you like best about being an architect?"

"What do you like least about scuba diving?"

"What advice do you have for kids who are interested in tropical fish?"

You'll want to bring your research notebook to the interview to jot down important ideas, but having a tape recorder along is a better way to get all the information that is discussed. If you don't own a tape recorder, you can check one out of the library or borrow one from a friend. Practice using your tape recorder ahead of time, so you won't be fumbling with it when you arrive for the interview.

Be sure to arrive on time and leave at the end of the

prearranged time. If the informant is "on a roll" and is enjoying the experience, she or he may ask you to stay longer, but it is up to the expert to extend the interview. Remember, the expert is doing you a favor by sharing his or her time and ideas.

If you need to find out certain dates or details about an event, don't be afraid to ask for more specific information. During the interview, encourage the informant to talk to you by paying close attention to his or her words. Maintain eye contact as much as you can, and speak clearly and loudly enough to make a good interview tape. While the person is talking, encourage him or her by saying things such as "Mhmmm," "Yes, I see," or "Uh-huh," so that he or she knows you are listening.

After the interview, write up your notes from the tape as soon as possible. Be sure to write down the date, location, and time of the interview, so that you can include it in the list of resources at the end of your research project. It is a smart idea to send a thank-you note soon after the interview. You may have to call the informant again to double-check on some of the facts, and the person will be more likely to help you if he or she knows that you appreciate the help.

The Real Thing, Part II—Secondary Sources

Most of the sources you find in the library are **secondary sources**. They are called secondary sources because the people who wrote or produced the materials may have used original or primary sources, but you are getting the information secondhand, told in the author's words and filtered through the author's eyes. Students doing research reports in middle school, junior high, or high school use mainly secondary sources, along with an occasional primary source. College students and professional researchers try to use primary sources as much as possible. A combination of primary and secondary sources usually provides enough information for an excellent report.

Try to think of the whole library when you are doing your research. Don't stop at the reference section, where the encyclopedias and atlases and almanacs are. Continue to search the library catalog for other works. Don't forget about the **biography** (books about people) section, the **periodicals** (magazines and newspapers), the **pamphlet file** (sometimes called the vertical file), and the **media materials** (films, videos, audiotapes, etc.).

As you discovered when you were scoping out your topic, magazines and newspapers (periodicals) contain a lot of information. Now is the time to track down the best periodical articles for your report. Copy the correct dates, volumes, and pages of each source from the *Reader's Guide, Magazine Index,* or a newpaper index.

Find the articles from the back issues of the magazines. Sometimes old magazine issues are bound together in large books and kept in a storage section of the library. Often past issues of some newspapers and popular magazines, such as *Time* or *Newsweek,* are stored on rolls of microfilm. Wherever they are, they will be stored alphabetically by the title of the periodical and organized by date. Many microfilm readers can also make a paper copy of the information you see on the screen.

After you've found as many of the articles as you can, decide which ones are best and find out if you can check out the magazines. Newspapers usually must remain in the library. Take careful notes or photocopy the article if you cannot take it home.

Let the Computer Do Your Searching

Another source to consider is **database searches**. Most public libraries now offer this service. Some school library media centers are beginning to do computer searches also. Here's how it works. Indexes to magazines, newspapers, and other information resources are stored in a big computer. Librarians use a computer, a phone line, and special software to tap into a large information bank. By keying in a research subject, the librarian can produce a printed list of articles in a matter of minutes. Of course, you still have to hunt for each article, just as you do when you use the print indexes such as the *Reader's Guide*.

Libraries have to pay to use these computer services. Because the libraries pay according to the amount of time they are connected to the computer service, the customer may be charged a fee as well. Ask about the fees and availability of the service at your local library. Computer database services can save you a lot of time.

Many libraries have also put their list of materials (formerly the card catalog) on a computer, and computer terminals are scattered throughout the library for anyone to use. There is no charge to use the library computer catalog, and usually it is user-friendly.

Chapter 3: Research Skill Activities

1. Identify someone in your community to interview. Think of questions to ask your informant and write them down in your research notebook.

2. Practice interviewing by asking a friend questions. Try to tape-record his or her answers. Consider the following questions:

"When were you born?"

"How many brothers and sisters do you have?"

"Where have you lived during your life?"

"What do you like best about your neighborhood?"

"Tell me about your travels to other states or countries."

"Describe what you do for fun. Explain your hobbies or interests."

"What are your favorite movies? books? TV shows? Why?"

Make up some questions of your own.

Pretend you are introducing your friend on a TV talk

show. Use the information that you have gathered to write a lively, fun introduction. Read your introduction to your friends.

3. Listen to an interview done by a professional reporter on TV or radio. What kinds of questions do they ask? Think about the qualities that make a good reporter.

4. Find out if your library or media center offers computer searches. How much does it cost? If there is no fee, ask for one on your research topic.

5. Is your library's catalog on computer? If so, how many listings can you find on your chosen topic? (If your library has a card catalog, how many cards can you find listing materials on your research topic?)

6. Make a list of the best articles you can find in magazines or newspapers. List at least four articles with:
- the name of the source
- the month, day, and year of the source
- the author of the article (if given)
- the title of the article
- the pages on which the article is published

Put a check next to the title of each article when you find it in the library. Put another check next to each title as you read the article.

44

4

Getting Ready to Write

By now you might be thinking that this research business is a lot of trouble and a lot of work. It *is* a lot of work, especially at first when you are getting the hang of it. But think of it this way—you're learning something about your topic and you're developing super skills at the same time. It's a good deal!

You'll need to get into the good habits of knowing how to find information, organize it, and present it in an interesting way. Many teachers rely on students knowing how to gather information and learn independently. The older you get, the more you will be expected to find the materials you need for learning on your own.

You never know when research skills will come in handy outside school. When you want to buy a new bike, or, later on, a new car, you'll want to be able to interview the salespeople, to read about the best model, and to survey your friends about their favorites. When you want to try a new hobby such as photography or raising rabbits, you'll be glad you know how to do research. Research is a skill you'll use for life.

Reading "Smart"

You have completed the hard part of research—finding sources. The rest of your project involves the nitty-gritty of sorting out the important ideas and facts and putting them together with your own unique view of the topic.

Now that you have the resources you need, you must find the nuggets of helpful information within them. Don't be overwhelmed by the stack of materials you've collected. Instead, start by scanning each piece to decide which portions you will read thoroughly.

Scan each book by looking carefully at the chapter headings in the table of contents or by looking up specific subtopics in the index at the back of the book. One way to find out if a chapter will be especially important to you is to read the first paragraph and the last paragraph in that chapter. The opening and ending paragraphs will sum up the author's ideas and should let you know whether or not you need that material in your report. Mark the important chapters with a removable piece of paper. When it is time for note-taking, you can easily see the sections you want to read carefully.

Use a similar method for magazine articles. Look at the illustrations. Then read the first and last paragraph of the article. Notice the section headings printed in bold print. You can mark specific places that catch your eye with slips of paper. If you've done a good job of selecting the magazine articles, you'll probably want to read each one thoroughly. Make sure to take complete notes about the sources you use. An article that doesn't seem important at first may become necessary later, when you're writing your paper.

Outline Time

Now it's time to go back to the outline map you made from your research questions. After scanning your materials and scoping out the research design, you probably have a better idea of the topics you want to cover in your report.

Take out your research notebook and look carefully at your original questions. What subtopics did you leave out? How would you change it now that you know what materials are available? Have you included too many subtopics? Make the necessary changes so that your outline becomes a real working plan from which you can write your report. The better your outline, the easier it will be to write the finished product.

Here is what a final outline looks like for a research project on the history of TV. Eric, the student researcher, wants to answer the following research questions: Who developed the first television sets? What was early television like? Why has television become so popular? What is the future of television? First Eric wrote an idea web about television topics. Then he developed a plan that included interviewing local television news anchorpeople, talking to other students about favorite TV shows, and doing library research on the history of TV.

After Eric did some browsing and scanned the sources he found in the library, he listed the main points he wanted to cover in his report.

Here's the outline he made to help him write the research report.

Outline: Television — Yesterday and Today

I.   Introduction
    A. TV's popularity today
    B. Different uses for TV
II. What is the history of TV?
    A. Early inventions leading to TV
    B. Radio communication to television communication
    C. First TV programming
        1. Comedies to news
        2. Commercials
III. How is television used today?
    A. Facts about TV sets and viewers
    B. Concerns about too much TV
IV. What is the future of TV?
    A. Videos
    B. VCRs
    C. Computers
V.   Conclusion—TV's short history has changed entertainment and communication

Each major point in the outline will become a main section in Eric's report. Each subpoint in the outline will become a paragraph or two. In one way, the outline is like a skeleton of the report itself, listing the important ideas that make up the meat of the research work. The outline might change after Eric completes his interviews and after he has tracked down all the information he needs.

The notes Eric takes when he reads his material or interviews people will provide him with the meat of the report.

How did Eric get from his outline to the final report? After he found his source material, he took careful notes on the cards in his research deck. He wrote down the author, the name of the article or work, the title of the source, the year it was published, and the pages where the article appeared. For exact quotations and facts, he carefully wrote down the exact page where the information appeared. He also wrote summaries of the information he read.

Taking Notes

You can create an excellent report by taking good notes from your resources. Three to four weeks before your research project is due, start taking notes from the books, magazines, and other media that you have gathered. There's no way that you can lay out the materials the night before the report is due and expect to write a good research report. It is just too big a project to do at the last minute. So get into the habit of taking notes carefully. By making just a few note cards a day, you'll have your report written before you know it.

It's best to write notes on the research deck (the 4" x 6" cards) that you have on hand. The 4" x 6" cards give you enough space to write quite a bit, and they're not as messy and hard to handle as paper can be. You can also move and organize cards easily.

There are two kinds of note cards—**bibliography cards** and **content cards**. Bibliography cards (**bib cards** for short) list a separate source on each card. The end of your research report will have a **bibliography** to let your reader know what books or other sources you used to get the information for your report. Some writers prefer to call this list a **mediagraphy**, a word that more accurately describes the variety of resource materials that you might use, including films, videocassettes, audiocassettes, printed material, and interviews. If you are using several nonprint sources in your research report, you will want to call your resource list a mediagraphy.

Each bib card should list the author of the source, the title, the place of publication, the publisher, and the year published. If you only used part of the work, list the specific pages used. It's also a good idea to include the call number of the book on your card, even though it isn't needed in your bibliography, in case you want to look up the book again. Here is a sample bib card for a book that Eric used in his report.

A-1

Cheney, Glenn Alan. <u>Television in American Society</u>. New York: Franklin Watts, 1983.
J791.45
C42
AA

The book's title is <u>Television in American Society</u>. Notice that the title is underlined. Titles of books, magazines, and films are usually underlined. This book was written by Glenn Alan Cheney and published in New York by a company called Franklin Watts in 1983.

The "A-1" at the top of the card indicates that this is the first card Eric made for this book. Eric gave this book the letter *A* because it was the first source from which he took notes. Each content card with the letter A means that the information came from the source listed on the bib card A-1. The bib card is always the first one. Card A-2 will have notes about the book's content. Eric will continue on A-3, if necessary, and on as many cards as he needs to complete his notes from source A. Putting the "A" at the top of the content cards saved Eric from having to repeat the name of the author and the title of the work on each card.

Each kind of resource is listed in a special form in a bibliography or mediagraphy. The bibliography gives readers enough details so that they can look up one of the books themselves.

Bibliography or Mediagraphy Formats

Here is Eric's list of resources that he included with his research report. (These formats are adapted from the recommendations of the Modern Language Association.)

Television — Yesterday and Today
BIBLIOGRAPHY/MEDIAGRAPHY

Booth, Stephen A. "Television—Past and Future." Popular Mechanics July 1989: 20-22.

Cheney, Glenn Alan. Television in American Society. New York: Franklin Watts, 1983.

Communication Primer, film. Dir. Charles and Ray Eames, 1953. 16 mm, 30 min.

Elwood, Ann, Carol Orsag, and Sidney Solomon. The Macmillan Illustrated Almanac for Kids. New York: Macmillan Publishing Co., 1981.

Fifty Years of Television: A Golden Celebration. CBS. WCCO, Minneapolis. 26 Nov. 1989.

Harpur, Patrick. The Timetable of Technology. New York: Hearst Books, 1982.

Information Please Alamanac, 1989. New York: Houghton Mifflin Co., 1988.

Lear, Norman. Personal interview. 17 Jan. 1990.

"Television." World Book Encyclopedia. 1988 ed.

"Television: The Box That Changed the World Still Shapes Our Views." American Baby May 1988: 80-84.

"The Video Revolution." Newsweek. 6 Aug. 1984: 50.

Content Cards

Content cards, as you have probably guessed by now, summarize the content of your sources. They are also used to write direct quotes. When you use someone else's ideas or their exact words, you must give that person credit by telling your reader what your source was. The author's name or the magazine title in parentheses in Eric's report tells the reader where he got the idea. For example, Eric writes:

"In fact, 98 percent of all homes in the U.S. have television sets (<u>American Baby</u>, 80)."

He is telling his readers that he found the fact in the magazine named <u>American Baby</u>, on page 80. The article did not have an author, so Eric listed the magazine title in the bibliography. When an author is given (such as Cheney or Elwood), he uses that person's names in parentheses to show that he got his information from books he or she wrote.

Sometimes researchers give credit to their sources by putting small notes at the bottom (or foot) of each page. These notes are called **footnotes**. Other researchers give credit at the end of a report, in notes called **endnotes.**

Authors work hard to create the exact words they choose. To use someone else's words without giving that person credit isn't fair—in fact, it is against the law. It is like stealing. To use someone else's words and pretend that they are your own is called **plagiarism**. Taking careful and accurate notes helps the researcher give proper credit when credit is due. That is why your note cards should include the exact page where you found the quotation, the statistic, or the idea.

Here are some examples of note cards that Eric made for his report.

Content card

A-2

There is concern about TV watching
—TV is very realistic
—so many people watch it
—millions of people share the experience
—people believe that what is shown on TV is true and
  is also important

Quotation card

A-3

"Printed material was the first mass medium, the first
means of communicating with masses of people."

p. 1

Here is the first part of a report on television that Eric
wrote from his outline.

Television — Yesterday and Today

It seems that just about every home in the United States
has a television set. Most people watch some TV during
the week. Programs range from news to soap operas to
music videos and more. In fact, 98 percent of all homes in
the U.S. have television sets (American Baby, 80). Television's
history is short, but TV is so popular that it will probably
have a great future.

Chapter 4: Research Skill Activities

1. Set a goal for yourself and decide how many note cards you will write each day. If you take notes on 2-3 cards each school day, by the end of 2 weeks, you'll have 20-30 note cards. At the end of a month, you could have 40-60 cards! How many note cards will you aim for each day?

2. Work on your research deck by creating five bib cards. Card A-1 will be an article from an encyclopedia. Card B-1 will be a book. Cards C-1 and D-1 will be magazine articles. Card E-1 will be a media source (a videotape, a film, a filmstrip, or an audiotape). Check with your teacher or librarian to see if you have written down all the information correctly.

3. Work on your first content card (A-2). Read the article in the encyclopedia carefully. Write down the major points or important facts. Remember that if you write down the exact words the author of the article used, you must put those words in quotation marks. Be sure to indicate the page where you found the exact words, so that you can give the author credit in your report. If you need more than one card, go on to create cards A-3, A-4, and so forth. Every time you find information or a quote about a new or different topic of your outline, start a new card. When you finish the encyclopedia content cards, you'll be ready to go on to B-2 in your research deck. B-2 will contain information from the book source you have found. Continue to take notes until you have gathered information from all of your sources.

56

5

Putting It All Together

Now it's time to put all your work together into a report. Look back at your idea web and your outline. This will remind you of the main points you wanted to cover when you began this project. Compare your outline with the research deck that you've assembled. If you have found additional information that you didn't know about when you made your outline, change the outline to include all the subtopics that you'll talk about in your report. In other words, revise your outline *now* so that you can work from it when writing your report. The more detailed your outline, the easier it will be to write your paper.

Organizing the Research Deck

Here's where your research deck will come in handy. Take all of your #1 cards (A-1, B-1, C-1, D-1, etc.), and put them in alphabetical order. For the most part, this means that you will be arranging the cards by the authors' last names. This group of bib cards will form your list of references at the end of your report.

Now go through your outline and pull out the content cards or the quote cards that give information about the different topics in your outline. To guide you through your report, write the code from the card (for example, B-2 or C-4) next to the topic that it fits in the outline. As you write the report, pull out the card with that information and include it in your report. Taking the time to organize your notes this way may seem like an extra step at first, but it will help you write your paper easily and clearly. If you have taken notes carefully and arranged them logically, the writing part will go along without much pain and strain.

Keep your research notebook and any cassettes that you made during your interviews handy. Look through the research notebook to refresh your memory about your topic. Listen to short sections of the interviews to bring back to mind your important findings.

Writing the Report

This is one place where neatness counts! Write a rough copy of your report (usually called a **draft**), then read through it to see if everything is correct. If you can, ask your mother or father or older brother or sister to look at the paper for any obvious mistakes in spelling or grammar. If your family has a computer and you can use a word processing program, your report will have a polished look that your teacher is sure to appreciate. When you are happy with your final draft, copy the report over in your best handwriting, typing, or word processing.

Here are some major sections that your final paper should have:

1. **Title page**. On the first page of your report, list the title, your name, and whatever other information your teacher requires, such as your class or grade, the date, and your teacher's name.

2. **Table of contents**. If your report is more than four pages long, your teacher may ask you to include a table of contents. You have seen a table of contents in books; now you can make one of your own. Be sure to include the major headings of your report, any illustrations or charts, and the bibliography or mediagraphy.

3. **The Body of the Report**. Use all the good writing practices you have learned to construct interesting sentences and well-organized paragraphs. Express your main points, then give the evidence that you have uncovered from your research. Use quotations, facts, and survey results to support your ideas. Remember to keep that research deck of note cards, bib cards, and quote cards handy.

4. **Illustrations**. Usually diagrams, charts, or illustrations come at the end of a report, but you can insert them within the body of your report.

5. **Bibliography/Mediagraphy**. Remember to list your sources in alphabetical order. Be sure to include all the publication information, such as the year a book or article was published.

A report cover will give your paper that polished look

of a job on which you've worked hard. Use a cover if you can. If you don't have time to get a cover, staple your report together to make sure that none of the pages are lost. Just in case the pages or cover come loose, number each page in the report.

You can now have the satisfaction of showing someone else all that you learned through your research. Congratulations on a job well done!

Tracking the Facts
Research Timeline

Week One   **Finding a Topic**

   Make an idea web
   Check the encyclopedia for subject categories
   Narrow your topic
   Map your research questions

Week Two   **Scoping the Project**

   Make a library visit:
      Find basic information in reference books
      Check the library catalog for other sources
      Browse for interesting books
      Find articles in periodicals
      Check the biography section
   Find people resources:
      Identify people to interview (informants)
      Make interview appointment(s)
      Decide if a poll or survey will be necessary
   Write the final research plan

Week Three   **Using Information Gold Mines**

   Find primary sources:
      Visit historical societies
      Conduct interviews

Find secondary sources:
  Make a follow-up library visit
  Locate and check out or photocopy library materials
Distribute a questionnaire or conduct a poll, if necessary

Week Four   Getting Ready to Write

Revise the project outline
Take notes from source material:
  Make bibliography/mediagraphy cards
  Make content cards
  Make quotation cards
Compile results from the questionnaire or poll

Week Five   Putting It All Together

Organize the research deck of cards
Write the card numbers you will use on the outline
Write a rough draft, following the outline and using the
  note and quotation cards
Check spelling and grammar
Write a final version
Put together any needed illustrations or charts
Make a list of resources used from the bib cards
Make a title page
Make a table of contents, if necessary
Number all the pages of the paper
Make an attractive cover and bind the pages into the
  cover
Pat yourself on the back!

Bibliography

The Diagram Group. *Handtools of Arts and Crafts: The Encyclopedia of the Fine, Decorative and Applied Arts*. New York: St. Martin's Press, 1981.

Dolan, Edward F. *The Julian Messner Sports Question & Answer Book*. New York: Julian Messner, 1984.

Gibaldi, Joseph and Walter S. Achtert. *MLA Handbook for Writers of Research Papers*. 3d ed. New York: The Modern Language Association, 1988.

Hollander, Phyllis. *100 Greatest Women in Sports*. New York: Grosset & Dunlap, 1976.

Lester, James D. *Writing Research Papers: A Complete Guide*. Glenview, Illinois: Scott, Foresman and Company, 1987.

Lolley, John L. in consultation with Samuel J. Marino. *Your Library —What's in It for You?* New York: John Wiley & Sons, 1974.

Lyttle, Richard B. *Jogging and Running*. New York: Franklin Watts, 1979.

Mabery, D.L. *Tell Me about Yourself: How to Interview Anyone from Your Friends to Famous People*. Minneapolis: Lerner Publications, 1985.

Mann, Thomas. *A Guide to Library Research Methods*. New York: Oxford University Press, 1987.

McInerney, Claire. *Find It! The Inside Story at Your Library*. Minneapolis: Lerner Publications Company, 1989.

Olney, Ross R. *The Young Runner*. New York: Lothrop, Lee & Shepard, 1978.

Sattler, Helen Roney. *Dinosaurs of North America*. New York: Lothrop, Lee & Shepard, 1981.

Index

almanac, 27

bibliography, 50, 52, 59
biography, 26, 40
brainstorming, 9-10
browsing, 22

call numbers, 22
computer searches, 41

databases, 41

encyclopedias, 15, 16, 20,
    21, 26
encyclopedia index, 16
endnotes, 53

film, 35, 40
footnotes, 53

idea web, 14-15, 16
interviewing, 27, 36-39

library catalog, 21, 42

magazine indexes, 24-25
mediagraphy, 50, 52, 59
microfilm, 24, 40-41

newspaper indexes, 26
note taking, 49-54

outline, 17, 47-48

periodical indexes, 24-26
plagiarism, 53
polling, 28
primary sources, 35-39

reference books, 15, 20, 22
research design, 19-31
research plan, 19-31, 29-30
research topic: ideas for, 9-10;
    narrowing the, 16; size of,
    11-14

secondary sources, 39-42
surveys, 28

videotape, 35, 40